Rookie Read–About® Science

Save the Rain Forests

By Allan Fowler

Consultants

Linda Cornwell, Learning Resource Consultant,
Indiana Department of Education

Fay Robinson, Child Development Specialist

Lynne Kepler, Educational Consultant

Children's Press®
A Division of Grolier Publishing
New York   London   Hong Kong   Sydney
Danbury, Connecticut

Project Editor: Downing Publishing Services
Designer: Herman Adler Design Group
Photo Researcher: Caroline Anderson

Library of Congress Cataloging-in-Publication Data

Fowler, Allan.
    Save the rain forests / by Allan Fowler.
        p. cm. — (Rookie read-about science)
    Includes index.
    Summary: Discusses the need to conserve the rain forests because
of their wealth of plant and animal life, effect on weather, and
importance to people throughout the world.
        ISBN 0-516-20029-1 (lib. bdg.) — ISBN 0-516-26084-7 (pbk.)
        1. Rain forests—Juvenile literature.   2. Rain forest conservation—
Juvenile literature. [1. Rain forests. 2. Rain forest conservation.]
    I. Title. II. Series.
    QH86.F685   1996   96-16972
    574.5'2642—DC20   CIP
                                                              AC

20 21 22 23 R 11   62

This is what you see when you fly over a tropical rain forest. From the air, you can't see the ground.

The ground is far below
that top green layer, called
the canopy.

A canopy is formed by the leaves on top of many tall trees. The trees grow very close together.

They are so close to each other that hardly any sunlight reaches the ground, or floor, of a tropical rain forest.

That's why there are only a few places where plants can grow on the ground.

Those few places, if they are thick with plants, are called jungles.

Yet a rain forest is filled with many kinds of plants, including ferns, mosses, and colorful orchids.

Since they can't grow on
the sunless floor, some plants
grow high up on the trees.

Sunlight reaches them there, and they get moisture from the air. Woody vines called lianas have roots in the ground, but climb way up.

Curtains of Spanish
moss hang from trees
in some rain forests.

This kind of forest is called a rain forest for good reason.

It rains most days — hard.

Thundershowers come often. A tropical rain forest is always warm, and usually quite hot.

You might say that the animals there live upstairs and downstairs. Mammals such as deer and tapirs live on the ground.

tapir

So do capybaras, the
world's largest rodents.

orangutan

Chimps and orangutans are at home on the floor or in trees.

So are wild members
of the cat family.

jaguar

Some animals spend their whole lives in trees — monkeys and lemurs, flying squirrels and bats . . .

fruit bats

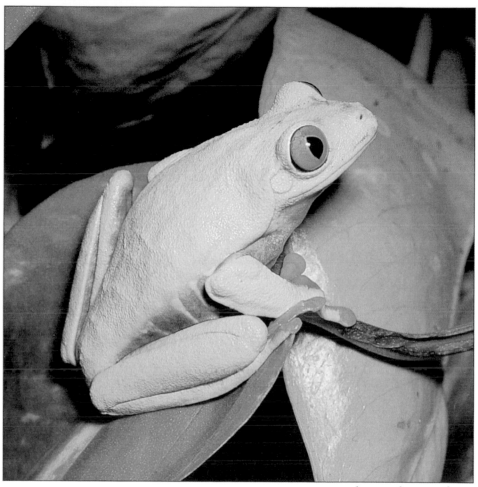

red-eyed tree frog

snakes, lizards, and frogs . . .

toucan

brightly colored birds such
as parrots and toucans.

Beautiful butterflies are among the many insects.

bromiliad

More different forms of life can be found in a rain forest than anywhere else — but very few people.

The soil in a rain forest is not good for growing the food crops that people need.

The green areas on this map show the world's tropical rain forests. Biggest of all is the Amazon River Basin, in South America.

NORTH AMERICA

At O

Amazon River Basin

SOUTH AMERIC.

Pacific Ocean

Every day, the rain forests are growing smaller and smaller.

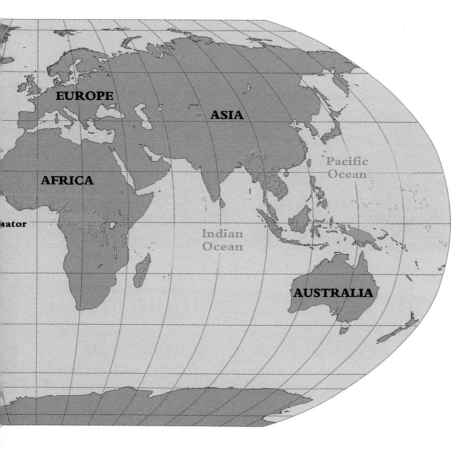

People are cutting them down.
They are clearing spaces for
new towns and farms.

They use the trees for
making furniture.

26

As their home forests are destroyed, many kinds of animals and plants vanish from the earth.

Many of those plants give us medicines that help cure sick people.

Some scientists believe
that when we cut down the
rain forests, it changes the
weather in other parts of
the world.

Now you know why people
say, "Save the rain forests."
Let's hope that the rain
forests with their great
richness of life are saved.

29

Words You Know

canopy

ferns

lianas

orchids

tapir

capybaras

flying squirrel

orangutan

Spanish moss

Index

About the Author

Allan Fowler is a free-lance writer with a background in advertising. Born in New York, he lives in Chicago now and enjoys traveling.

Photo Credits

Comstock — 9, 31 (top middle), 13, 31 (center right), 14, 31 (bottom middle), 26; ©Boyd Norton, cover; ©Sharon Chester, 8; ©Franklin J. Viola, 16

Photo Researchers, Inc. — ©Jacques Jangoux, 3, 25, 30; ©Stephen J. Krasemann, 7 (inset), 31 (top right); ©John Eastcott/YVA Momatiuk, 29

Visuals Unlimited — ©H.A. Miller, 4; ©Jon Bertsch, 7 (background), 31 (top left); ©Richard Walters, 10, 31 (bottom right); ©S. Maslowski, 31 (bottom left)

Valan Photos — ©Ken Cole, 12, 31 (center left), 15; ©John Mitchell, 17; ©John Cancalosi, 18; ©Bruce Lyon, 19; ©Paul J. Janosi, 20; ©Y.R. Tymstra, 24;

©Herman Adler Design Group — 22-23

COVER: Rain forest in the Amazon Basin, Ecuador